The Lambourn Valley Railway

Charles D'Arvelle

Website - www.BretwaldaBooks.com
Twitter - @Bretwaldabooks
Facebook - Bretwalda Books
Blog - bretwaldabooks.blogspot.co.uk/

Bretwalda Books
Unit 8, Fir Tree Close, Epsom,
Surrey KT17 3LD
info@BretwaldaBooks.com
www.BretwaldaBooks.com
ISBN 978-1-909099-74-6

CONTENTS

CHAPTER 1
BEFORE THE RAILWAY

People have been living in the Lambourn Valley since at least the Bronze Age, and probably back into the Neolithic some 5,000 years ago. They were attracted by the proximity of the high downs where livestock could be grazed to fertile valley lands where agricultural crops could be grown and reliable springs where cool, fresh water bubbled up from the chalk.

From 1850 onwards there were some dramatic changes to farming in the valley. Cheap imports of grain from North America meant cereal farming was no longer profitable. Cheap wool from Australia undercut sheep farmers on the downs and even dairy farmers found themselves less prosperous than they had been.

Despite these problems the Lambourn Valley was still a pleasant place to live. Even if some farmland had gone out of production and been turned over to woodland or rough pasture. The number of inhabitants remained steady and they continued to work the land, or for those in the lower valley to work in Newbury. There was plenty here to tempt a company to build a railway, but the Lambourn Valley had one advantage that similar rural areas did not - racehorses.

The turf here was softer and springier than it was at Newmarket or Epsom, then the two major centres for horsebreeding and training. Some horses found the hard going at Newmarket and Epsom rather harsh for their delicate joints, and their owners recognised that they would do better if trained at Lambourn. Those promoting a railway to Lambourn knew that the race horse owners would pay good money to have their horses taken out of the valley by rail.

It was not just horses that drew the LVR to Lambourn. If the upper downs were ideal for horses, the lower lush pastures were ideal for cattle, prime young steers that could be slaughtered for meat, leather and other products. The journey by road was lengthy and tiring for cattle and farmer alike. Both would benefit if they were taken out by rail. The second major product of cattle at Lambourn was milk. Taking milk out by train meant that that milk from cows milked in the early morning in Lambourn could be taken by train to London in order to be on sale in time for the morning shoppers. The farmers would gain a new and more lucrative market for their milk, and the LVR would have another profitable freight.

The economic case for a railway up the Lambourn Valley did not rely solely on exports. Imports were important as well. The most important of these was coal for nearly all domestic heating and cooking was done on coal fires. But coal was heavy, so transporting it was expensive. The coal for the Lambourn Valley had to come by horse and cart from Newbury and the further up the valley it went the more expensive it became. Transporting coal by rail would be much cheaper.

Finally the LVR anticipated making money from passengers. In the later 19th century very few people owned horses, and those that did used them for working on farms or for haulage. The only realistic options open for most people wanting to travel anywhere were to walk or go by train. The going rate on railways for passenger travel was 1d per mile for Third Class, 1 1/2d for Second Class and 2d for First Class. Spending a penny was preferable to walking for 20 minutes, especially in poor weather, so passengers could be expected to use the LVR. The building of a railway massively increased the number of people travelling. Commuting to work was not something that anybody had done before the railways, and as late as the 1890s almost nobody in the Lambourn Valley commuted at all. Once the railway was opened, however, people commuted to Newbury to work, and some went further afield.

Racehorses on a practice ride over the Lambourn Downs. It was the promise of freight traffic associated with the horseracing business that was a major attaction for those promoting the construction of a railway up the Lambourn Valley. Photo: Philipjelley.

CHAPTER 2
THE LAMBOURN VALLEY RAILWAY

In 1873 a proposal was made to extend the Newbury town tram system up the valley all the way to Lambourn. The Mayor of Lambourn, the Earl of Craven, ceremonially hammered in the first spike at Cheap Street. But then the tram company got cold feet and the scheme was never completed.

Also in 1873 the Didcot, Newbury and Southampton Railway was founded to link those three towns. The plan called for a branch line to run from Shaw, just north of Newbury, up the Lambourn Valley to Lambourn. The residents of Shaw objected most strongly and the idea was dropped.

The two failed schemes had, however, convinced local businessmen that a railway up the Lambourn Valley would be a paying proposition. The Lambourn Valley Railway Company (LVR) was formed in 1882 with Mr. G.B. Eyres as

Lambourn village lies in a hollow in the Berkshire Downs near the head of the Lambourn Valley. Photo: philipjelley.

Chairman, Mr Walter Money as promoter and Mr Baldry as Engineer. The following year the necessary Act of Parliament was obtained and work began.

On the basis of a preliminary survey of the route, Mr Baldry produced the following estimated costs of construction.

Purchase of land ...	£10,000
Excavation and embankments ...	£10,083
Works, including rail at 59lbs per yard ...	£27,273
Stations, signalling etc ...	£10,712
Giving a total estimates cost of	£58, 068.

Estimates were one thing, getting the work done proved to be quite another. Two railway engineering companies put in bids for the works specified in the survey. Kirk & Parry offered to do the work for £60,000 and were willing to take £12,000 in shares in the LVR. Furners & Baldwin said they would do the work for £82,000, taking £30,000 in shares. After much discussion, the directors of the company opted for the more expensive bid from Furners & Baldwin.

On 6 November 1884 the LVR began raising funds, offering shares for sale at £10 each. The company prospectus painted a rosy picture of rapidly increasing transport demands in the Lambourn Valley leading to healthy income and profits. Interest in Newbury and the Lambourn Valley itself was intense and in just two months a total of 2,365 shares had been sold. Local worthies were taken on as directors and shares were being sold nationally, though they went only slowly outside of Berkshire.

Over the next couple of years detailed survey work was undertaken. Mr Baldry left as Engineer and was replaced by William Gregory. In 1888 Furness & Baldwin relinquished the construction contract, apparently due to disputes over the new survey work. The contract was relet to Billups of Cardiff. The deal with Billups was rather unusual in that the LVR agreed to pay only £18,000 in cash, with £30,000 being paid in shares and another £33,000 being borrowed from Billups themselves.

Among the problems that was increasing the cost of construction was the precise route the new railway should take out of Newbury. The town was expanding and flat land near the town was rapidly increasing in price. It had already been agreed that the LVR would terminate at the GWR station in Newbury, where a dedicated platform for the use of the LVR alone was to be built. After lengthy discussions with the GWR, the board of the LVR agreed to the following arrangement.

The GWR would build a bay platform on the north side of Newbury Station that would be conterminous with the Up Platform. They would also build a single track line for the LVR to run alongside the GWR lines west out of Newbury and across West Fields to a point 1,000 yards west of Newbury Station where the tracks of the LVR would diverge from the GWR lines. For this work the GWR would charge the LVR £6,000 and there would be an annual charge of £25 for the use of the bay platform and £50 a year for the use of the tracks across West Fields.

Construction of the LVR lines north from the GWR lines was complicated by the fact that the ground was soft and, in places, marshy. Moreover an embankment was needed that would be high enough to lift the line up to cross first the Kennet and Avon Canal and then the River Kennet by bridge. A heavy girder bridge was installed sitting on brick abutments. Beyond the Kennet there was a hill rising to 35 feet above the river, and this required a cutting to be put in that was bridged by a road bridge carrying the main London-Bath Road (now the A4). Beyond the hill was the Lambourn, where another bridge was needed. These proved to be expensive engineering works.

In June 1890 some 4.5 miles of the line had been completed, but work came to a sudden stop. The LVR directors accused Billups of Cardiff of substandard work and stopped paying the bills, so Billups stopped work. The case eventually reached court in May 1891. The court found for the LVR, and ordered Billups to hand over all materials and equipment plus £1,000 by way of compensation. Work did not start again until 1897 when a new contract was given to Pearson and Son. The line was eventually finished in the spring of 1898.

The railway was laid as a single track line all the way from Newbury to Lambourn. At 12 miles and 32 chains, this made the Lambourn Valley Railway one of the longest stretches of single track in southern England. At Newbury the line ended in a bay platform, No.3, and there was a loop to allow the engine to pull the train into Newbury, then decouple and get to the other end of the train ready to pull it back to Lambourn. The layout at Lambourn was rather more complex as it was here that the rolling stock were stored and based. There were no loops or sidings at any of the intermediate stations.

The track was composed of flat-bottomed rails spiked directly on to wooden sleepers, then placed on to ballast. The steepest gradient was 1:60, which occured near Newbury where the railway had to get through a cutting in Speen Hill. The track was laid in as straight and level a route as possible, with the sharpest bend

*The LVR locomotive Ealswith stands at the LVR's bay platform at Newbury.
Steam is up and the train is ready to depart down the line toward Lambourn.*

being one of 20 chains radius. Because there was only a single track it was decided that signals were superfluous. There was to be only one train on the line at any one time, so collisions were impossible. Another saving was made by not installing a telephone line along the railway. On other lines it was usual by the 1890s to link the stations by phone so that the stationmasters could advise each other of any problems, delays or other news relevant to the running of the railway. The directors of the LVR felt they could do without a telephone line, again as only one train would be in operation at a time.

No railway was allowed to open or operate without a safety approval by the Board of Trade. For the LVR this inspection was carried out by a Colonel Yorke on 31 March 1898. He found everything to be in order, but chose to impose a couple of restrictions on the operation of the line. No train could travel at faster than 25mph, and no carriage or freight wagon could be loaded to an axle loading of more than 8 tons. The company agreed and Colonel Yorke signed the certificate allowing the line to open.

Always on the look out for a way to reduce costs, the board of the LVR applied in 1902 for their railway to be reclassified as a Light Railway by the government under the terms of the Light Railways Act of 1896. This Act defined a Light Railway as one that operated at a maximum speed of 25mph on straight track and 8mph on bends, and that had a maximum axle loading of 12 tons. Since the LVR already met two of these three criteria the directors needed only to reduce speeds on the few bends to 8mph to comply.

The advantages of being reclassifed as a Light Railway were considerable. Business rates payable on the stations were less than for a standard railway, moreover level crossings did not need to be protected by gates, but only by cattle grids and signs, and nor did the level crossings need to be permanently manned. There were similar savings to be made in terms of staff levels and a variety of technical details in all of which criteria for a Light Railway were lower than those of a standard railway.

The Board of Trade held a new inspection of the line, followed by a hearing in March 1893 that was held in Newbury. The hearing was open to anyone who wished to raise any objections. There were a few questions regarding safety, but these were all answered satisfactorily and the Board of Trade approved the conversion of the LVR into a Light Railway.

Directors and Staff

The Lambourn Valley Railway (LVR) was the idea of a group of businessmen in Newbury and the surrounding area. The idea was that the construction of a railway up the valley would ensure fast and reliable transport links from the villages to the outside world. This would, the promoters believed, boost the local economy and give themselves a healthy profit. A good idea all round.

The first Chairman of the Board was a Colonel George Branston Eyre of Welford Park. Eyre was a serving army officer, but seems to have been partly retired for he spent much of his time at home. It was he who provided the necessary information and engergetic lobbying to get the Lambourn Valley Railway Act through Parliament in 1883. He addressed the public meeting held in Newbury Town Hall on 6 November 1884 that launched the company to the public. Mr Eyre gave a very positive view of the project, supported by other promoters Walter Money and Henry Holmes. He stated that no less than 25,000 people would be served by the new railway, assuming that anyone within an hour's walk of a station would use that station for transport. He estimated that the cheaper and faster transport would make about 60,000 acres of land currently used for grazing or left waste economic to farm. He also presented financial figures that showed the company turning a decent operating profit from its first full year of operation. He ended up by announcing that shares in the new company would be sold at £10 each. This was a considerable sum then for most working men would be lucky to earn £4 a week. Clearly the venture was aimed at the middle classes.

The pitch by Mr Eyre worked well and soon 2,365 shares had been sold to people in Berkshire. This was not enough to construct the entire railway, but it was enough to get going. A Mr Baldry was hired as Engineer for the works, though he stayed only three years before being replaced by Mr William Gregory.

In 1892 the Chairman of Board of the LVR ceased being George Eyre and became George Archer-Houblon. In fact the two were one and the same person. Eyre had inherited a vast fortune from a cousin, but on condition that he change his name to perpetuate the family of Archer-Houblon. This he happily did and although he was a frequest visitor to his new lands in Essex he remained living at his own family seat at Welford Park. He became a Justice of the Peace and patronised the local good causes. He was, however, a man of unusual energies and still found time for the LVR, a project ideal for his administrative abilities and energetic spirit.

Archer-Houblon now decided to restructure the finances of the company by rewriting the articles to allow the company to borrow money, not only raise cash through the sale of shares. He then got authorisation from the Board of Trade for four alterations in the route that would reduce construction costs. Finally he persuaded Parliament to amend the Act of 1883 that, among other things, gave the company an extra four years to finish building the line.

Archer-Houblon's next move was to open talks with the Great Western Railway. The LVR already had a good relationship with the GWR. The LVR line ended at Newbury, where the GWR was building a special bay platform with loop for the Lambourn trains. Archer-Houblon now floated the idea that the GWR might agree to run the trains along the finished line. This arrangement was one that the GWR and other large railway companies had entered into with several other small, independent railways. It allowed the smaller company to retain ownership of their line and to make decisions about timetables and rolling stock. It also allowed them to take advantage of the expertise of the larger company in running trains and finding reliable railway staff. The usual arrangement was for the income from tickets and freight to be divided between the two companies. The GWR took the proposal seriously and in 1895 a draft agreement was drawn up between the two companies.

In the event the operating agreement with the GWR did not materialise, so the LVR had to run its own railway. Archer-Houblon launched a vigorous search for good men, and seems to have been advised informally by the GWR who had a strong interest in making the new line a success.

The General Manager was the first to be hired. He came in the shape of Mr W.H. Gipps who took up the post as a part time appointment. He was already Traffic Manager for the Didcot, Newbury and Southampton Railway, another independent line that linked to the GWR at Newbury, and he seems to have worked out of Newbury to the benefit of all three companies. Mr. J.S. McIntyre now took over from William Gregory as Engineer, while Henry Holmes took up post as Secretary and was responsible for the general administration of the business.

At the last minute there was a possible disaster when the LVR could not afford to pay for either locomotives or rolling stock. No manufacturing company was willing to let the LVR have equipment on hire purchase, perhaps because the new company was known to be in some debt. Archer-Houblon stepped in again. Out of his own pocket he bought two locomotives, four passenger carriages and an assortment of freight wagons. He then entered into a hire-purchase agreement with the LVR that would see him recoup his investment and the LVR eventually own the locomotives and rolling stock.

Once the railway was up and running, Archer-Houblen felt he could take things a bit easy. He remained as Chairman of the Board, but in 1902 Mr J.B. Squire was hired as Managing Director. The move was prompted partly by the fact that Mr Gipps was suffering from ill health. In July 1903 Mr Gipps died, to be mourned by all who knew him. His place was taken by Mr Sidney Woodley.

The new arrangements of senior staff and management was thrown into turmoil on 21 January 1904 when the GWR contacted the Board of the LVR and offered to buy them out for £50,000. The AGM of the LVR was due in February and the offer was put to the shareholders. The details of the discussions were not recorded, but Archer-Houblon was re-elected as Chairman while Henry Holmes resigned as Secretary and was replaced by Mr G. Whitelaw. Archer-Houblon's first act after his re-election was to politely decline the offer from the GWR.

In January 1905 the GWR tried again. This time they proposed an amalgamation, not a takeover. The debts of the LVR would be paid off by the GWR, while shareholders would either be paid in cash or GWR shares. The details of the deal are complex, but it would seem that the shareholders of the LVR were making a slight loss on their initial investment. The Board of the LVR travelled by train up to Paddington to the plush offices of the GWR for final talks. The details of this meeting were then taken back to Newbury for a Special General Meeting of the LVR held in May 1905. The new deal from the GWR was accepted, and there then followed a vote of thanks to Colonel Archer-Houblon for all his work for the company. It was passed unanimously. On 1 July 1905 the deal took effect, and all that was left for the LVR was a final board meeting on 19 July to agree the final, formal business. Thereafter the LVR became part of the GWR.

The Locomotives and Rolling Stock
Problems raising the necessary money and disputes with the building contractors meant that the railway was not completed until 1898. As the line neared completion the directors of the company turned their attention to finding

The locomotive Ealswith at Lambourn Station shortly after it was delivered. The locomotive is hauling the four original passenger carriages.

locomotives to work the line. They already owned a small engine that had been used by the building contractors to haul rails, sleepers and other construction material from Newbury as the line was built, but this was not really suitable for hauling real trains.

In January 1898 the board selected a pair of locomotives manufactured by the Avonside Engine Company of Bristol and priced at £1,165 each. Avonside was a leading locomotive manufacturer which had formed in 1864 by a merger of a number of smaller engineering works. The company specialised in smaller locomotives, supplying a large number of clients both in the UK and abroad. They specialised in the manufacture of saddle-tank engines, with the 0-4-0 configuration being a particular favourite of Avonside.

Unfortunately the LVR did not have the cash to pay in full for the two engines. Talks aimed at payment by installments broke down and the LVR faced the uncomfortable prospect of opening their railway without having any locomotives to operate it. The GWR was appraised of the problem and stepped in to help.

The GWR had recently taken over the Watlington and Princes Risborough Railway in Buckinghamsire. Along with the railway it had acquired a 2-4-0 tank engine built by Sharp, Steward and Co. of Glasgow in 1876. The GWR had no real use for the engine and were happy to hire it to the LVR for a modest fee. The LVR, of course, had to supply the driver, fireman and cleaner as well as all the coal, oil and other consumables. On 2 April the hired engine proudly pulled the inaugural train from Newbury to Lambourn, stopping twice, in a time of 37 minutes.

The hiring of the 2-4-0T could only be a temporary solution. The timetable of the LVR really required two engines so that one would always be in steam. Within days of the line opening the LVR signed a contract with Chapman and Furneaux of Gateshead to purchase two locomotives for £1,330 each. The LVR still did not have enough money to pay for the locomotives, but Chairman of the Board Archer Houblon bought them and rented them to the LVR.

The two locomotives were identical 0-6-0 side tank engines with outside cylinders and inside frames. The wheelbase was set at 9 foot 6 inches and each wheel was 3 feet 7 inches in diameter. They had domed boilers measuring 8 foot 0.5 inches by 3 feet 2 inches and containing 113 tubes each 1.6 inches in diameter which gave a heating surface of 447 square feet. The tanks held 550 gallons of water and the fuel hopper 42 cubic feet of coal. The working pressure was set at 150lb per square inch.

After some consideration the directors decided that the engine livery of the LVR should be dark blue with black lines edged in white.

The board also decided that their two engines should be given names, not numbers. With a fine sense of history they opted for the names "Alfred" and "Elyswith". The names were taken from Alfred the Great, King of Wessex, and his wife. The Lambourn Valley had been part of Wessex when Alfred ruled, but more to the point he had won a battle at a place called Ethandun, which may well have been Edington a few miles west of the Lambourn Valley. A later board meeting changed the spelling of the names to "Aelfred" and "Eahlswith" which was closer to the original Anglo-Saxon.

Aelfred arrived on 15 October 1898, with Eahlswith being delivered a few days later. Both were put to work and the hired 2-4-0T returned to the GWR. The GWR promptly sold it to the Weston Clevedon and Portishead Railway. That railway was an independent light railway primarily involved with stone from quarry to dock for export, but it did carry passengers as well.

Back in the Lambourn Valley the problems were not yet over. As was usual a proportion of the money had been held back until the locomotives had been run in and accepted as working properly by the LVR. Unfortunately Aelfred suffered a series of minor problems, the most serious of which was an intermittent habit of running warm. Archer Houblon wrote to Chapman and Furneaux stating that the outstanding £660 would remain unpaid until the problems were sorted out. Presumably they were for the money was paid a few weeks later.

By 1903 the increase in traffic had persuaded the board of the LVR that a third locomotive was needed. Chapman and Furneaux had in the mean time gone bankrupt, so a new locomotive builder had to be found. The Hunslet Engine Co. of Yorkshire proved willing to be paid in installments that could be afforded by the LVR itself. For a sum of £1,255 Hunslet agreed to produce a 0-6-0 side tank locomotive very similar to Aelfred and Eahlswith. This locomotive was to be named "Eadweade" after the son and successor of Alfred the Great.

The new engine was slightly larger than the other two. The wheels were the same size, but the wheelbase was 10 feet 6 inches. Again the working pressure was identical, but the boiler was larger. This gave it a weight of 14 tons, as opposed to 23.5 tons.

Little more than a year after Eadweade arrived the LVR decided that it needed to make economies. Among these was the replacement of the steam locomotives for passenger trains with steam railcars. These improved operating efficiency, but

15

required a new inspection of the line by the Board of Trade as they had an axle weight of 12 tons, more than was authorised on the LVR. The line passed the new inspection and the railcars began operation.

The three locomotives were put up for sale. All three were bought by the Cambrian Railways, which had recently been formed by the amalgamation of a number of smaller railways in central Wales. The Cambrian ditched the names and gave the locomotives numbers. In 1922 the GWR took over Cambrian and so became owners of the ex-LVR locomotives. No.820 (Ealhswith) was sold in 1931 to work at a colliery in Somerset and then scrapped in 1945. No.821 (Aelfred) was likewise sold to a colliery, this time one in Glamorgan in 1933. It was scrapped in 1942. The longest survivor was No. 819 (Eadweade) which continued to run on the GWR until April 1946 when it was finally scrapped.

Archer-Houblon decided that the only way to get any rolling stock at all on to the LVR was for him to pay for it himself. The arrangement was not entirely altruistic, for Houblon-Archer then lent them to the LVR under a hire-purchase

A GWR steam railcar. In 1904 the LVR it introduced steam railcars hired from GWR to work the line for a while, but they were later replaced by a variety of smaller steam locomotives.

agreement. So long as the LVR kept up payments to Archer-Houblon, to be funded from passenger tickets and freight revenue, then the carriages and wagons would eventually become company property.

Archer-Houblon approached Brown, Marshalls and Co Ltd of Birmingham for the carriages. This company had been founded in 1840 and specialised in producing small carriages at low cost for smaller railways, they also produced narrow gauge stock. Archer-Houblon ordered four identical carriages, all of which arrived in time for the railway's opening.

Each carriage was 26 feet 6 inches long and was mounted on four wheels by means of leaf springs. At either end was an open platform with steps going down on either side. These were essential on the LVR as the platforms were barely 9 inches tall. The platforms also had an opening, usually closed off by a chain, that gave access from one coach to the next. Again this was essential for the LVR as it allowed the guard to walk right along the train from one end to the other selling tickets to those who had boarded at an unmanned halt.

All the carriages were divided into First Class and Second Class seating, though there was no internal partittion between the two. The two types of seating were entered by separate doors. The First Class seating was plushly upholstered and all seats were sprung and cushioned. First Class seating on the LVR was every bit as comfortable as on the larger railways.

The same could not be said of the Second Class. In fact the designation was something of a misnomer for the seating was the equivalent of Third Class on most other railways. The floors were bare boards, the seats were plain wooden slat benches without either cushions or upholstery. On the plus side, however, the fares charged by the LVR for their "Second Class" was much the same as prices for Third Class elsewhere.

The differentiation between Second and Third Class seating at this date has often been misunderstood. While First Class seats were generally used by the gentry, Second and Third Class were used interchangeably by everyone else. Third Class accommodation was composed mostly of bare wood as it was used by workmen going to and from work in their dirty working clothes. Mud, coal dust, grease and goodness knows what else adhered to these clothes and rubbed off on to anything they touched. Thus Third Class seats needed to be easy to wipe clean. Those same workmen would use Second Class when travelling in their normal clothes, perhaps taking the wife and children on a day out or visiting relatives. Second Class was composed of padded and upholstered seats, albeit of a lower quality than in First Class. That the LVR carried only First and Second (in reality Third) Class seating was more a reflection of the need to save money on rolling stock than on the social profile of the villages along the valley.

For goods wagons, Colonel Archer-Houblon turned to two sources. The GWR let him have six second hand wagons for £91 10/6d. He also bought another 12 second hand wagons for £189 from the Metropolitan Railway Carriage and Wagon Co. Ltd of Birmingham. This company made wagons and carriages for a variety of railways. Archer-Houblon ensured that he purchased a good mix of wagon types so that freight of any kind could be carried on the LVR. What all these wagons had in common was that they were four wheel wagons. This made them cheap to buy and were perfectly adequate for use on the slow LVR, though they would have been no use if hitched to faster trains on a mainline railway.

It was with this mixture of second hand wagons that the LVR began service. Soon afterwards the hired GWR engine was dispensed with and Archer-Houblon bought a pair of locomotives to run the LVR. These were named Aelfred and Ealswith after Alfred the Great and his wife.

In 1905 the LVR ceased to be an independent railway and merged with the GWR. The locomotives were sold, but the carriages and wagons were taken over by the GWR. These were not retained for use on the LVR. Instead the large white letters "LVR" were painted out and the wagons repainted in standard GWR design. Thereafter the line was home to a variety of GWR carriages or wagons. The GWR linked the LVR to the GWR at Newbury, allowing rolling stock to be used on the LVR as and when needed.

Operating the LVR
The first ever train into Lambourn Station from Newbury arrived on 2 April 1898. The journey had taken 49 minutes, and on board were the Board of the Lambourn Valley Railway Company. Two days later the train came back again, this time packed with shareholders and specially invited guests. Among these was William George Mount, MP for the Newbury Constituency which included the Lambourn Valley. He had come to open the line officially amid much public rejoicing and newspaper coverage. The station was decorated with flags and bunting, as was the train. A band played and people cheered.

The train then made two more round trips, this time with tickets available to the general public. Both trips were packed with not a seat to be had. Everyone in Lambourn wanted to have ridden the railway on the first day it came to town.

The directors announced that the timetable would be as full as could be achieved on a single-track line of over 9 miles with only one engine in steam. Including all the stops, it took a train almost an hour to get from one end of the line to the other. This meant that the first timetable had five trains running each way each day, but on Sundays there was an extra train each way in the late evening. All these trains would carry passengers, but the first morning train and two afternoon trains would also have freight wagons attached. The mid-day train in both directions did not stop at Stockcross & Bagnor, Welford Park nor at Eastbury. These were the least busy stops on the line, so the directors must have thought that folk heading to those village could wait for the next stopping train.

By October 1898 the LVR had acquired two engines, and the timetable changed accordingly. There were still five passenger trains daily, with a sixth on Sunday, but now none of these also carried freight. Instead there were three freight trains daily, with one in the early morning to collect milk churns left on the platforms by the dairy farmers of the valley. In addition the Saturday mid-day train now stopped at all stations, and on other days it would stop on request.

In its first full year of operation, 1899, the LVR clocked up an impressive total of miles run. In all 36,944 miles of passenger traffic and 5,598 freight miles were run. Even so there were continuing financial problems as the income generated barely covered the operating costs and debt repayments. The hoped for substantial profits for the shareholders did not arrive, and dividend payments were slow and intermittent.

In an effort to boost income the LVR introduced a number of concessions and excursions. The most successful of these was a day trip from Newbury to Uffington. Passengers were collected at Newbury early in the morning and taken up the LVR to Lambourn. After a stop for refreshment, the passengers were loaded on to horse-drawn buses and taken up the Ashbury Road (now the B4000) for a scenic drive over the high downs. The bus then turned to Uffington, arriving in time for lunch (included in the price) after which there was time to visit the famous White Horse of Uffington. The more energetic tourists could blow a blast on the Blowing Stone. This large boulder was pierced by a number of holes, one of which behaved like a trumpet if blown hard enough. It was said that Alfred the Great had blown on this Blowing Stone to muster his men to march against the Viking invaders. Then it was back on the bus to return over the downs to Lambourn. There the train was boarded to return to Newbury.

By arrangement with the GWR it was possible for passengers to buy through tickets for this tour from any GWR station. Some enthusiastic travellers came from London. So popular was this tour that it was repeated several times.

Profitable as such excursions were, they were not enough to secure a solid profit. In 1902 the timetable was reduced to four passenger trains each way daily, with two of them hauling freight wagons as well. This allowed the elimination of one of the freight-only trains in the afternoon. The fifth passenger train still ran on Saturdays and Sundays, but the sixth Sunday service was also cut. The changes reduced costs and increased profits, but unfortunately they also increased complaints.

It soon transpired that the majority of complaints were not so much about the reduced number of trains as the changes to when they ran. A particular grievance was that the first train the morning from Lambourn to Newbury had been moved

The Blowing Stone at Uffington. When the right hole is blown through hard enough the stone emits an eerie and surprisingly loud trumpet-like sound. Photo: ballista.

from 7.40am to 8.15am. This meant that several workers who had used the 7.40am to get to work were now arriving late. The LVR rapidly shifted the timetable yet again so that there was a train leaving Lambourn for Newbury at 7.45am that called at all stops.

The GWR brought in its own rolling stock, men and managers. Over the years that followed the GWR gradually replaced the distinctive LVR features with its own and by the 1930s there was little to differentiate the once independent Lambourn Valley line from any one of a dozen other GWR branch lines. Among the most significant improvements made by the GWR was to link the LVR lines to the GWR mainline at Newbury. This made it possible to run through trains from Lambourn past Newbury to Oxford. The line prospered.

After the GWR took over the line and carried out its varied improvements and changes it altered the timetable again. Real efforts were made for the first time to ensure that the trains on the Lambourn Branch connected smoothly with trains at Newbury that were running fast to London, Oxford and other major destinations. Not only that but some of the Lambourn trains became through trains that passed through Newbury to go on to other destinations. This was made possible by the GWR putting in a link from the Lambourn line to their own mainline. Oxford and Didcot were the most popular destinations for these through trains, but the occasional changes to the timetables made during GWR ownership meant some went further afield.

The good times could not last for ever. In 1930 a bus route was opened from Newbury to Lambourn, following the road that ran alongside the rail line for most of their route. The GWR hit back by finding ways to cut costs. In 1936 the Lambourn line was chosen as the venue for the experimental use of a diesel railcar. The test was deemed a success so in 1937 the GWR bought a diesel railcar specifically for the Lambourn route. This was fitted with buffers and drawgear to haul vans or trailers up to a weight of 60 tons, and had seating for 49 people. It could manage a top speed of 45mph, though this was rarely reached on the Lambourn branch and could develop 242bhp.

It was not long before the drivers on the Lambourn line recognised a potentially serious problem with the driver's window on the new railcar. The window was shaped in such a way that the driver could not see the couplings from his seat. The only way to keep an eye on the couplings was to stand up, which made it very difficult to control the foot throttle. Inevitably there were some severe jolts when coupling up and although nobody was hurt they became a real feature of the Lambourn line. By 1938 the GWR had introduced a special goods train that ran down and up the Lambourn line after the last passenger train of the evening.

Sucessful as the Lambourn Valley Railway was, it began to suffer a similar decline in profitability as did other rural lines.

During the 1930s a bus route was opened from Upper Lambourn to Newbury. This called at all the villages served by the LVR, ran more frequent services - especially on market days - and was cheaper. Inevitably passengers began using the bus more often than the railway. At the same time the profits to be made from shipping coal also began to decline as houses switched to electricity and gas

If these trends were visible in the 1930s they accelerated in the 1950s and were joined by others that also impacted on the LVR. The surfaces of rural roads improved dramatically as most lanes received tarmac coverings. These made the ride much smoother, and safer in inclement weather. Together with improvements to the reliability and suspension of goods lorries this meant that transporting goods by road became a viable proposition. Milk, vegetables, livestock and even skittish racehorses were all being moved by road by the later 1950s. The economic underpinnings of the LVR had been taken away and the end was soon in sight.

In 1947 the GWR and other railways in Britain had been nationalised to form British Railways. In December 1959 British Railways announced that the

A GWR diesel railcar. These were introduced for the less busy branch lines such as the Lambourn Valley to save costs and keep the lines profitable.

Lambourn line would close from Welford Park to Lambourn on 4 January 1960. The evening train that day was the last to run out of Lambourn Station. Two years later the lines were lifted and the station site put up for sale. Freight trains would only go so far as Welford Park.

In 1965 the British Railways freight services to Welford Park came to an end, leaving only the trains running to the American air base on the line. In 1972 the USAAF announced that it too would be turning to road transport. The line to Welford Park and the station were abandoned. In 1975 the tracks between Newbury and Welford Park were lifted.

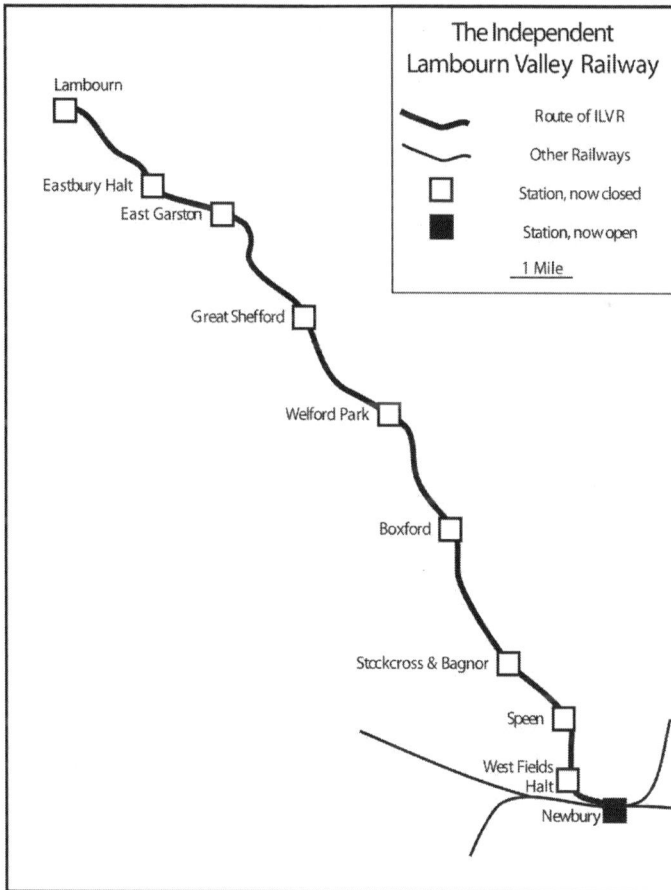

The route of the Lambourn Valley Railway from Newbury to Lambourn showing the intermediate stations and track route as of 1920.

CHAPTER 3
THE STATIONS

Newbury West Fields

The station of West Fields Halt stood, as its name suggests, on what were once open fields to the west of Newbury. The area is flat and low-lying, so the fields were mostly meadows beside the River Kennet that flooded in particularly wet winters. The West Fields were given over to grazing and haymaking.

The railway line from Newbury to Hungerford ran straight across the West Fields, slicing them in two. The building of the line necessitated the draining of much of West Fields so that they no longer flooded in winter, and the land went over to agricultural use. In later Victorian and Edwardian times the town began to spread, though this was mostly north of the river. As yet the built up area was not expanding much into West Fields.

Neither the Great Western nor the Lambourn Valley built a station at West Fields, but when the GWR boughtout the LVR they decided to open a new station closer to Newbury. The company chose a spot barely 100 yards north of where the LVR lines diverged from the GWR. The halt that was constructed consisted of a single platform with a standard GWR shelter and staffed by a single man.

At this date the station stood in empty fields and it may have seemed an odd place for a station, but as so often the GWR knew what it was doing. Soon a number of houses were being built. There was quite a mix of housing. There were a few good sized villas for middle class families, plus a larger number of semi-detached and terraced cottages for less prosperous folk. Soon the new West Fields Halt was busy with men commuting to work in Newbury, or changing trains at Newbury to go on to work elsewhere.

The new station was fairly simple, consisting of a single platform with a shelter to give passengers a break from inclement weather. The main access to the station was off Craven Road, though a gate gave access to a path leading to Clifton Road. A third path led straight across the tracks to allotments. One assumes that the allotment holders had to be careful when crossing, at least no accidents were ever reported. This station was the only one on the entire LVR that had gas lamps to illuminate the platform - all the others had oil lamps. A gas main was close enough to give a link.

In 1955 a study found that on an average weekday 16 people boarded a train here and 16 people got off again, presumably they were the same people. Ticket sales totalled £17 5/7d for the year, while maintenance costs were £30. It was decided to cut back maintenance to the bare minimum.

In 1956 Newbury West Fields was removed from the railway timetables, though trains continued to stop here for locals to hop on or off. In 1957 it was found that the shelter needed replacing, but ticket sales would not cover the costs, so the station closed.

A waiting room of the type installed at Newbury West Fields Halt by the GWR in 1906. This example is made of the usual wood with a metal roof, but that at Newbury West Fields was unusually of concrete.

After the closure of Newbury West Fields Halt, the people living in the adjacent roads lost their commuter line to Newbury and stops to Oxford. This did not stop them getting to work, however, and most now walked or took the bus to Newbury where those going further afield got the train. Building of houses in the West Fields area continued apace and in the 1990s a new cul-de-sac, Lipscombe Close was built over what had been the track linking Newbury West Fields Halt to Russell Road, one of the residential roads of terraced cottages built after the GWR opened the station in Edwardian times. The site of the actual Halt is now occupied by a footpath running from Lipscombe Close down to the towpath that runs alongside the Kennet and Avon Canal.

Speen for Donnington Station

The villages of Speen and Donnington lie on opposite banks of the River Lambourn, just a couple of miles from its confluence with the River Kennet. Speen is the older of the two, originating as the Roman settlement of Spinae in about AD100. A spring just north of the church is known as Ladywell and it is thought to have been sacred to a pagan goddess before it was taken over by the Christian faith and rededicated to the Virgin Mary. The church itself was built in about 900, though it has been largely rebuilt in medieval times. The church is mentioned in the Domesday Book of 1086, where it is named as "Spone" and recorded as being owned by Humphrey Visdeloup along with a mill.

Donnington does not appear until the middle ages, but rapidly grew to be larger and more prosperous than Speen. The wealth was founded on wool, produced by sheep grazing the downs and processed in Donnington and Newbury before being exported to the continent.

In the 1380s the spot attracted the attention of Sir Richard Abberbury. Sir Richard was Chamberlain to Queen Anne, wife of King Richard II, and was high in favour at court. Among the extensive lands that Sir Richard had inherited was the manor of Donnington. In 1386 he used his contacts at the court to persuade King Richard to give him a licence to crenellate, that is permission to fortify what was until then Donnington Manor and turn it into Donnington Castle. Such permission was hard to come by as no medieval king wanted to allow fortresses in private hands to spring up around the kingdom to hamper his ability to rule. Clearly Sir Richard was fully trusted by King Richard.

The resulting castle was to be one of the strongest in Berkshire. It was built on a roughly square plan with a round tower at each corner and a massive gatehouse dominating the entrance. The strength of the castle is demonstrated by the fact that for more than 250 years after it was built nobody dared to attack it.

In the 18th century Newbury became a busy stopping off point on the coaching routes from Bath to London. Donnington enjoyed a short-lived existence as a fashionable place for the richer travellers to spend the night. For a while the famous dandy and fashionista Beau Brummell lived in the village. But when the Great Western Railway built its mainline from London to Bristol to the north, Newbury's coaching trade vanished. The GWR later came to Newbury, but again both Speen and Donnington were bypassed.

All that changed when the Lambourn Valley Railway was built. The station that the LVR built at Speen for Donnington was, like all their stations, simple in form and function. The platform was less than a foot tall and served more to keep the surface dry in wet weather for the benefit of passengers' shoes than anything else. Passengers at Speen for Donnington had to climb up steps to get into the carriages.

After the GWR took over the Lambourn Valley Railway it began a programme of alterations to make the formerly independent line more consistent with GWR practice. The smaller stations including Speen for Donnington were rebuilt to match GWR style, as shown here at the Didcot Railway Centre.

Perched on the platform was a small shelter where passengers could wait in inclement weather. There was also a rather grandly named "office". This was by way of a small wooden shed with a window that could be folded down to act as a ticket window. The station was in the custody of a lone man who was ranked and paid as a Junior Porter, though in truth he was station master here and was expected to carry out all the tasks of a station master, albeit at a very quiet station.

The station was built adjacent to what was then the Lambourn Road. This left the Great West Road just to the south, then curved west to head up the valley. The presence of the road necessitated the construction of a level crossing. This too was in the hands of the Junior Porter and must have been his main worry. The road was quickly renamed Station Road, with Lambourn Road being retained as the name for the road after its sharp bend west.

The importance of safety was rammed home to the LVR in tragic fashion on 8 April 1898, just a few days after the line opened. It was Good Friday and a train had just left Speen for Donnington and gone through the tunnel under the Great West Road. As the driver emerged back into the daylight and finished traversing the bend he was horrified to see a group of children on the line. He leapt to the whistle, but it was too late. Two of the children, boys aged 11 and 13, were knocked down.

The shocked driver sent one of the survivors to run for a doctor, but it was too late. Both boys were taken to hospital, but died later that day. The line was closed temporarily, but was soon open again. At the coroner's inquest that followed it emerged that local children had taken to playing on the steep slopes of the cutting. Since the cutting had been completed more than a year before the line opened the area had become something of an informal playground. Although parents had warned the children that the line was about to open, the children had still gone to play there. The coroner ruled the deaths were accidental and found that the safety procedures of the LVR were adequate, though he did have some stern words to say about the importance of making sure they were properly enforced.

Thereafter Speen for Donnington settled down into a comfortable routine. The trains came and went, passengers alighted and boarded. The Junior Porter did quite well with tips from the richer passengers heading to and from weekends at the grander houses in Donnington. He may have had to struggle with the heavy trunks, but usually got a silver coin by way of reward. One or two of the wealthy residents were even known to slip him a golden sovereign at Christmas.

As the board of the LVR had originally foreseen, freight traffic was a major source of revenue. At Speen for Donnington it was livestock that were grazed on the adjacent water meadows of the Lambourn and Kennet that provide most of this traffic, along with coal for the homes of the two villages. Milk from nearby farms was another regular cargo. The sight of milk churns lined up on the platform awaiting the first train to Newbury and Oxford was a familiar one in the early mornings.

When the GWR took over, the platform was raised to a more usual height and a more comfortable passenger shelter installed. The station was also renamed, becoming simply "Speen" though for some reason GWR timetables continued to use the old name for another 20 years. The member of staff was upgraded from being a Junior Porter to being a Porter Grade 1. His working hours were extended so that he had to be on duty at the station from 7am to 8pm, though he was not expected to do much work other than when trains were due when he had to operate the level crossing and deal with passengers and freight.

In 1907 the GWR installed a phone linking all stations along the line. This made the job of the Porter at Speen considerably easier. Previously he had had to keep a close eye on his watch in order to be ready to clear the level crossing for the train when it came into earshot. Now the porter at the previous station phoned him to tell him when the train was leaving.

In 1934 the GWR made great efforts to save money on the Lambourn Branch. Most stations were stripped of both staff and signalling. The single line meant that signalling was usually redundant in any case and passengers could always buy tickets from the on-board guard. At Speen the presence of the level crossing meant that the member of staff was retained so that he could operate the gates, but the signalling was done away with.

The Speen staff porter could not take things easy with the declining amount of traffic. There were now no members of staff at either Newbury West Fields nor at Stockcross & Bagnor. They were now the responsibility of the man at Speen who had to visit them daily to keep them clean and tidy, and inspect the premisis for any problems. He also had to go to his other stations if requested to do so to help a passenger or with goods. The station finally closed in 1964 and the tracks were lifted soon after.

The site of the station itself is now occupied by a house and some workshops. Just to the south is a small cul-de-sac containing three houses. The builders decided to call this street "The Sydings", presumably as it lies off Station Road. Ironically there never were any sidings at Speen for Donnington.

29

Stockcross and Bagnor Station

The station of Stockcross and Bagnor lay about midway between those two villages, and some 2.5 miles northwest of Newbury. .

Before the railway came, the two villages led a fairly quiet and uneventful existence dominated by agriculture. Of the two, Bagnor is the older village. It lies down in the valley where the small Winterbourne Stream enters the Lambourn from the north. As its name suggests, the Winterbourne flows only in the wetter months of the year. There is a weir on the Lambourn just west of the village centre and it was probably here that the medieval mill stood.

For centuries Bagnor belonged to Westminster Abbey, which sold it in 1871 to a rich businessman from Newbury. The estate was later broken up and the various houses and farms are now in private hands. Stockcross, by contrast, lies on a hill some 60 feet above the river meadows. It was named for the stocks that stood beside the crossroads here, allowing petty criminals to be exposed to public view and contempt at a busy crossroads. It was not until 1839 that the village gained a church and a school, both paid for by the vicar, the Rev. H. Majendle.

The line from Newbury passed through Speen Hill by way of a cutting and a short length of tunnel that took the railway under the Great West Road (now the A4). The line then turned northwest, following the edge of Speen Hill to keep as level a course as possible. There were a few stretches of cutting and embankment on this section, but generally the route was kept level to reduce the costs of construction.

About a thousand yards from Speen for Donnington the line crossed Chapel Road, running from Stockcross to cross the Lambourn at the hamlet of Woodspeen and so reach Bagnor. The company decided to put a station here that would serve the two villages. At first the station was called simply "Stockcross" but within a very short time was renamed "Stockcross and Bagnor" to make it clear to those unfamiliar to the area that they could reach Bagnor via the Lambourn Valley Railway and that this was the station to use.

The lane ran through a sunken gully here, so the line was put up over it by way of a bridge. The station was placed on the west side of the lane where it could be constructed on the same level as the line. A short access drive was constructed from Chapel Road up to the station. As with all LVR stations, economy was important. The station consisted of a short, slightly curved platform built only 9 inches above the ground. This served to ensure that passengers kept their feet out of the mud on wet days, but little else.

West of Stockcross and Bagnor, the line dipped very slightly at 1:61 gradient to reach the banks of the Lambourn and then resumed its gentle climb up the valley.

The station was from the start in the hands of a single member of staff who was ranked as a Junior Porter, presumably to save on wage costs. He was on duty at the station all day, however, and was expected to carry out all the tasks of a station master, albeit at one of the quieter rural stations on a quiet rural line. In the wake of the conversion of the LVR to a Light Railway, Stockcross and Bagnor lost its member of staff and became an unmanned halt. If any passenger or freight was going to need staff assistance, the stationmaster from Boxford was expected to trot over to lend a hand.

Apart from some changes in the locomotives and rolling stock calling at this station, not much changed with the arrival of the GWR. In 1934 the station stopped featuring on timetables, though the trains still stopped here by request. After the Second World War the line was nationalised along with the rest of the GWR to form part of British Railways. The station closed in 1965.

There is not much to see of Stockcross and Bagnor Station today, but the site is easy to find. Chapel Road connects the B4000 to the Lambourn Road that runs

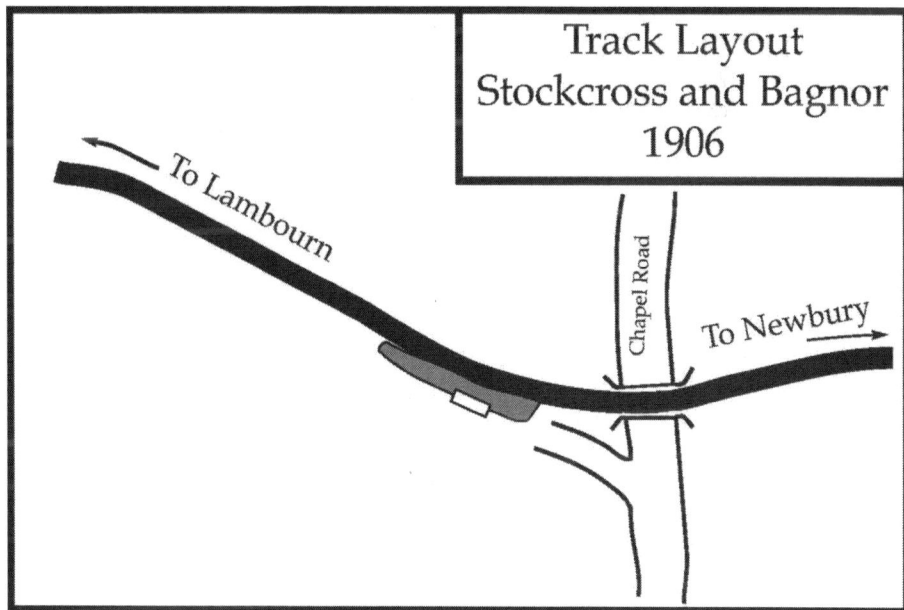

Track Layout
Stockcross and Bagnor
1906

To Lambourn

Chapel Road

To Newbury

up the Lambourn Valley from Newbury to Lambourn. About 200 yards south of Lambourn Road the open fields are interrupted by a dense line of trees and dense undergrowth. These mark the route of the abandoned railway. At Chapel Road the old embankments are a conspicuous feature as they crowd in on either side of the lane.

The station lay just west of the lane, on the south side of the railway line. The site is now occupied by a sloping field laid to grass for pasture and there is no public right of way giving access. From the lane the site can be seen clearly as it was just to the right of a telegraph pole on the top of the slight rise.

Boxford Station

The village of Boxford, for which the station was named, stands on the banks of the River Lambourn, the far side from the station. Strictly speaking the station stands in Westbrook, but that is a tiny hamlet and presumably the directors of the line thought more people and freight would want to go to Boxford. As so often when it came to naming a railway station the demands of commerce took precedence over geographical accuracy.

Boxford is one of the oldest villages in Berkshire. Archaeologists have found Bronze Age artifacts here, plus pottery from the time of the Celts who lived here when the Romans arrived. A large Roman building was excavated, but poorly recorded, in the 19th century just east of the village and villagers frequently turn up Roman pottery and coins when gardening.

The 19th Century was something of a boom time for Boxford. Many of the charming thatched cottages that today make this such a picturesque village were built or enlarged at this time and Boxford House, a notable mock-Gothic manor house, was put up. While the entire Lambourn Valley suffered from the depression in agriculture that struck England in the 1870s, Boxford suffered less than most and was recovering by the 1890s. It may have been this that encouraged the directors of the Lambourn Valley Railway to put a station here.

The line from Newbury cut through Speen Hill by way of a cutting and tunnel before entering the Lambourn Valley. It then ran northwest through the stations of Speen for Donnington and Stockcross and Bagnor. From the latter the line dropped slightly to reach the valley floor, then ran alongside the western bank of the stream as it climbed gradually upstream.

Just north of Boxford the Lambourn describes a large loop to the east, so to save distance the railway line cut through the edge of Rood Hill. To minimise the size of the cutting, the railway approached the hill on an embankment across the watermeadows. Boxford Station was built on the patch of level ground where the embankment reached the hill slope and before the cutting began.

As first built, Boxford Station consisted of a single platform built on the west side of the single track line. The platform was built to be less than a foot tall and was slightly curved to conform with the bend formed by the line as it turned slightly west to enter the cutting. There was a rudimentary wooden shelter for passengers to escape inclement weather.

Also occupying the shelter was the single member of staff, who had a lean-to store room in which to keep parcels, raincoat and other items. Ranked as a Junior Porter, this man was a general factotum. He welcomed passengers, helped them with any luggage and assisted the train crew with loading and unloading freight. He also kept the platform swept and tided up the footpath that gave access to the station from Boxford and Westbrook. Among his other duties, the porter was expected to deliver parcels to houses in Boxford village. He was given a company bicycle for the task.

In 1904 a new member of staff arrived in the shape of local man Charlie Brown. For the next 36 years until his retirement in 1940 Charlie Brown was the human face of Boxford Railway Station. He was also in charge of Stockcross and Bagnor as that station was left unmanned after 1940. He was not expected to be in two places at once, however, and went down to Stockcross only if he was told in advance that a passenger or some freight would need his help in some way.

When the GWR took over the platform was entirely rebuilt to be a more normal height, allowing passengers to step straight on to trains instead of having to climb steps to do so. On the platform the old LVR shelter for passengers was retained, while a new office was built for Charlie Brown plus a store for freight. A loop was added to the east side of the line. This was the first loop out of Newbury and was to be used as a passing place. In fact the loop was to be used more often as a siding than for its designated purpose. Also added by the GWR was a storage shed in which track maintenance gear was kept.

In 1926 the General Strike came to Boxford Station in an unusual form. Charlie Brown obeyed the call from his union to go on strike. He dutifully locked up the buildings at Boxford and went home. But he was also a special constable so he found at home a summons to report to Newbury Police Station for special duties during the strike. Switching uniforms, Charlie walked into Newbury. He found that the chief concern of the local police chief was an anonymous threat by unknown strikers to vandalise railway equipment and buildings left unmanned by strikers. Charlie was therefore promptly sent back to Boxford to guard the station where he would have been were he not on strike.

With Charlie Brown gone, the member of staff at Boxford became Edith McCartney. Despite inheriting Charlie's rank as Porter 1st Class, she insisted on being called "stationmaster". She was not expected to work into the evening, so once the 5.20pm passenger train to Newbury had departed she went home. In 1947 the post-war Labour government nationalised the railways, so the line became part of British Rail.

Passenger numbers continued to decline and in 1954 it was decided to do away with a full time member of staff at Boxford. Mrs McCartney obtained the post of Porter (again she insisted on Stationmaster) at neighbouring Speen instead. From there she came daily to Boxford to tidy up and check all was well.

There is not much to see at Boxford, and what there is stands on private land to which there is no public right of way giving access. However, the site can been viewed from a public footpath running from Westbrook to Weston by way of Rood Hill. To find this path you need to leave Boxford on Winterbourne Road and cross the River Lambourn. About 100 yards west of the river, Winterbourne

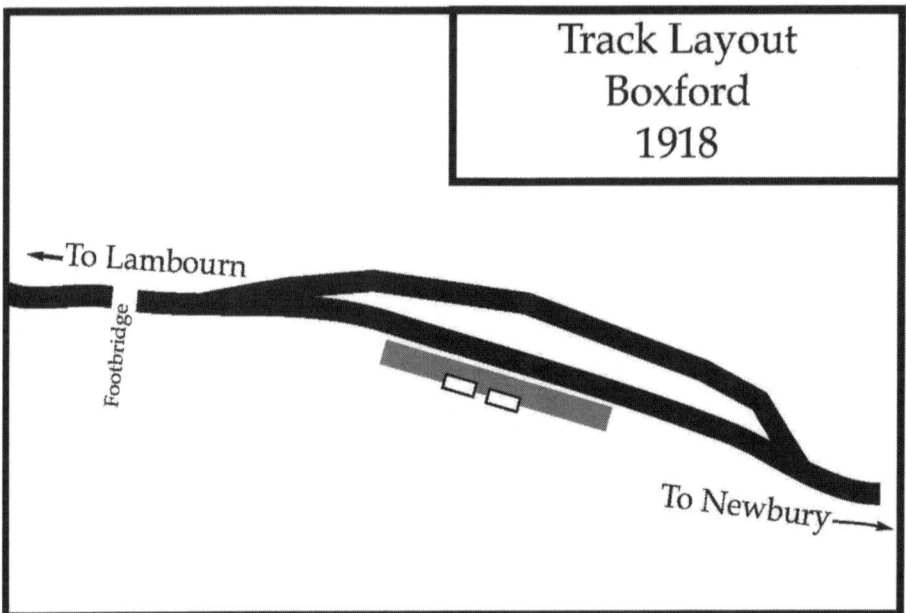

Track Layout
Boxford
1918

To Lambourn

Footbridge

To Newbury

Road takes a very sharp left hand turn where Westbrook Lane peels off to the right. Straight ahead of you is a flight of steps climbing a bank to join a footpath that heads off between two tall hedges that border the gardens of houses on either side. Follow this path for 50 yards until it suddenly emerges from the hedges and leaves the houses behind. In front of you are open fields. The site of the station lies about 150 yards north of this path. You get a better view in winter when the leaves are not on the trees, but even in high summer the site can be glimpsed.

Welford Park Station
The village of Welford sits beside the River Lambourn at a point where hills crowd in to make the valley floor narrower than it is elsewhere. Locals have found Roman coins and broken pottery near the village, though no excavations have been undertaken. The place first enters the written record in the 10th century when it is recorded as being the proprty of Abingdon Abbey.

The Abbey built a grange here where the monks could supervise their estates in the area, collect rents, store produce and generally ensure that the Abbey was getting its dues from the local farmers. When King Henry VIII closed down the monasteries and abbeys of England he grabbed the Grange at Welford for himself and converted it into a hunting lodge. His daughter, Elizabeth I, was less keen on hunting so she granted the converted buildings to Sir Thomas Parry. It remained in the Parry family until 1618 when it was sold to Sir Francis Jones, a wealthy London merchant who was looking for a country seat not too far from his business. In 1652 his son Richard demolished the old medieval building and put up a grand new residence which, with modifications, remains there to this day.

By the 1870s Welford Park, as the new grand house was known, was in the hands of George Eyre, soon to be Chairman of the Lambourn Valley Railway.

The line from Newbury cut through Rood Hill just north of Boxford by way of a cutting. It emerged from the north face of the hill at a steep 10 foot drop down to the River Lambourn. The railway was carried the 50 yards to the river on an embankment, then over the river on a girder bridge to another stretch of embankment that ran across the water meadows on the far side. The line then curved east to run along the hill opposite at a height above the valley that meant that neither embankment nor cutting was needed.

The line was now on the north bank of the Lambourn for the first time since leaving Newbury some five miles to the south. The line now had a gradient of 1:75, reflecting the gentle nature of the terrain going up the valley. The route followed the curve of the hill until it arrived above Welford and Welford Park. This spot was about halfway from Newbury to Lambourn and of rather more importance to the history of the railway was home to George Eyre, Chairman of the Board who lived at the house of Welford Park. For this reason the station was named "Welford Park" and not "Welford" after the village.

The original station erected by the LBV consisted of only a simple platform not even 12 inches tall and a wooden waiting room that doubled up as station office and storage for light freight. It was manned by a sole member of staff who was the rank of Junior Porter. Although most of his duties were those of a porter - assisting passengers and handling freight - he was also expected to keep the station clean and tidy, trim back bushes and generally make the place presentable.

One of the biggest freights to use Welford Park was watercress. The enterprising farmers of the village had flooded several of the meadows up river of the village to form wide, shallow pools that were ideal for growing this tasty green delicacy. It had not really been practicable to grow watercress here when the only way to get the stuff out was by slow horsecart. But with the new railway the watercress could be on sale in London's Covent Garden less than three hours after being picked, and you can't get much fresher than that.

Since Welford Park Station was the midway point along the 9 mile line the GWR decided on taking over the line to make substantial changes to the station. The track was dualled through the station and for some distance to the west. This allowed for trains to pass each other, or for spare wagons to be parked up on one of the lines. A crossover linked the two lines immediately west of the station. In the station itself there were two platforms, each with a waiting room. This made Welford Park the only station on the entire line that had both an Up and a Down platform. A booking office was located just beside the western end of the northern platform.

In 1943 Britain was at war with Germany and there was a huge demand for the training of pilots and air crew. Less than a mile to the northeast of Welford Park Station there was a stretch of chalk downland that was large enough and level enough to hold an airfield. The main purpose of what became RAF Welford was to take already trained pilots, air gunners, navigators and flight engineers and wield them into bomber crews that were competent to fly combat missions over Germany. Accommodation was mostly in the form of nissen huts as the base was not intended to be permanent, but was for the duration of the war only.

Welford Park Station was suddenly busier than it had ever been before. Large

Welford Park consists of the grand house which stands beside the parish church. The village of Welford lies a short distance away.

numbers of construction workers poured through the station, while vast quantities of building materials were unloaded here to be hauled up the hill to the site of the base. As the construction drew to an end, the workers were replaced by RAF personnel - both men and women - who came to their new home by rail. Those lucky enough to get a pass rushed out through Welford Park Station to head for the comparatively bright lights of Newbury for entertainment.

Soon after it was completed, RAF Welford was handed over to the 9th Air Force of the USAAF. The familiar RAF uniforms were replaced on the platforms of Welford Park by crowds of men and women in the uniforms of Britain's Allies. The American authorities used the base for highly secret missions and so for security reasons dubbed the station "Station AAF-474". This proved to be a less than catchy name for the personnel, so they quickly began calling the base after the railway station that they used to get to and from the base. Thus AAF-474 was more widely known as "USAAF Welford Park".

When the war ended in 1945 the RAF reoccupied RAF Welford and decided to keep it. In 1947 the base was put into "care and maintenance", meaning that it was not used but was kept in a useable condition. In 1953 it was announced that the Americans were coming back, and that meant great changes at Welford Park.

The new unit to be based at RAF Welford (this time the base kept its British name) was the 7531st Ammunition Squadron. This was primarily a transport unit that was tasked with keeping the many squadrons of the USAAF based in Europe fully supplied with weaponry. Some of that weaponry was big and heavy, meaning that the most suitable way to transport it safely was by rail. Construction workers moved in to build a network of standard-gauge light rail tracks around the base, but it was also decided to build a dedicated branch line from the air base to Welford Park. From there trains could go down the Lambourn Branch to Newbury and so access the national rail network.

Work on the new branch line was begun in 1953 and completed in 1954. The line diverged from the existing lines about 200 yards south of Welford Park Station, veering off to the north. The gradient on the branch line was fairly steep, even though the line curved right around north of Westbrook in order to climb up to the downs and the air base.

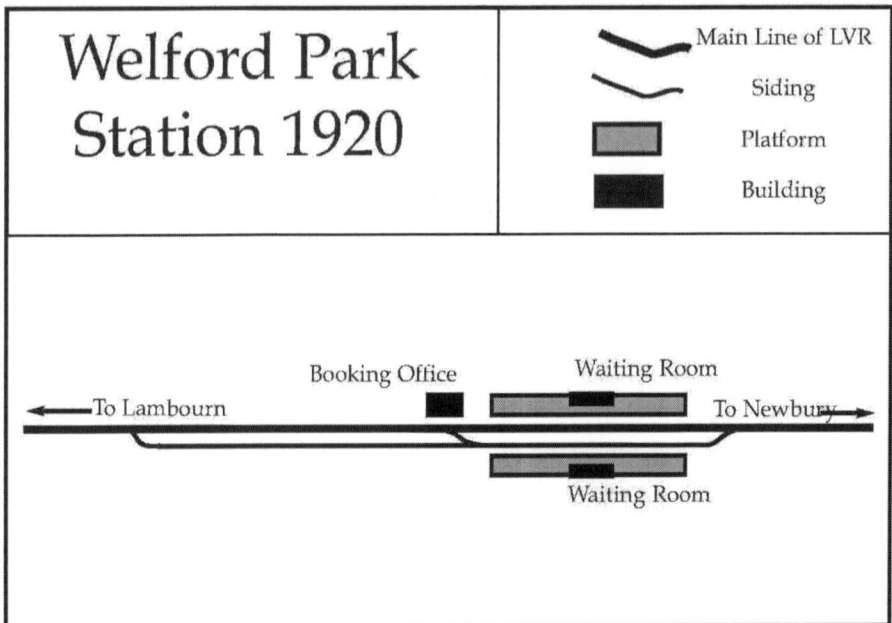

Welford Park Station 1920

Main Line of LVR
Siding
Platform
Building

To Lambourn
Booking Office
Waiting Room
To Newbury
Waiting Room

By the nature of the military needs, the trains bound for the base were dedicated trains run entirely separately from the usual trains operating up and down the branch line. These specials ran when there was a need for them, putting an extra load of work on to both the staff along the branch line and on the men working it. The specials came up the branch line to Newbury and pulled into Welford Park. They then reversed direction back toward Newbury to take the branch line up to the air base. Although the American trains were carrying heavy loads of high explosives there were never any accidents.

In 1959 British Railways announced that the Lambourn line north of Welford Park was to be closed entirely. The line south of Welford Park would be closed to passenger trains and freight only would run up to Welford Park. It was only the military trains that made the line at all profitable. In 1962 the lines from Welford Park to Lambourn were lifted, killing any hopes that the line might be reopened.

The coal merchant, L.J. Bodman and Sons, who supplied coal throughout the Lambourn Valley had previously had their main depot at Lambourn Station, but now moved to Welford Park. They took over what had been the goods yard.

In 1965 the British Railways freight services to Welford Park came to an end,

The site of Welford Station as it is today, looking east from the site of the dual track section, now used as a car park for Welford Park. The trees are growing on the platforms while the trackway is visible as a less overgrown path between them.

leaving only the American trains running on the line. In 1972 the USAAF announced that it too would be turning to road transport. The line to Welford Park and the station abandoned. In 1975 the tracks between Newbury and Welford Park were lifted.

There is rather more to see at Welford Park than at other stations along the old Lambourn Valley Railway. The buildings here were rather more substantial than elsewhere. To find the remains, leave Welford and cross the Lambourn to find a crossroads. Turn left or northwest up the Newbury Road towards Lambourn. The site of the station was about 200 yards from the crossroads, set back to the right hand side of the road. The site is now used as an overflow car park for those visiting Welford Park and can be accessed whenever the gardens are open to the public. The two platforms remain and can be picked out fairly easily. The platforms themselves are now overgrown with bushes, scrub and young trees. Here and there timber revetments can still be seen sticking out, covered in moss and rotting away. The trackbeds are less overgrown and provide easy foot access. None of the wooden buildings survive.

Great Shefford Station

The station of Great Shefford was originally named West Shefford and was built to serve the three Sheffords - West Shefford, East Shefford and Shefford Woodlands. These villages were for centuries inextricably linked to the mighty Fettiplace family, many of whose members are buried in the church at East Shefford. Shefford Woodlands stands two miles to the southwest up on the downs and astride an old Roman road. As its name suggests the hills here were once heavily wooded, and some extensive stands of timber remain.

The largest of the three villages is, however, Great Shefford. This village was known as West Shefford until the decline of East Shefford left it as the most populous of the three. The name of all three villages derives from the term "Sheep Ford", which commemorate not only the fords over the Lambourn at both West Shefford and East Shefford, but also the vast numbers of sheep that once roamed the downs above the villages.

The line from the GWR station at Newbury cut through Speen Hill to reach the lower Lambourn, then ran up the valley staying as close as possible to the river to take advantage of the shallow gradient and avoid the need for expensive cuttings and embankments. The halfway point was at Welford Park Station. From there the line ran northwest on the north bank of the Lambourn to reach East

Shefford. Just before the village the lines ran over the main Oxford-Hungerford road, now the A338, before reaching a patch of flat land where the Great Shefford Station was built. The station was accessed by a path from the main road.

The original station that opened in 1898 consisted of a single platform lying on the west side of the line as it curved slightly. There was a basic wooden shelter for the use of passengers in wet weather, and this had to double up as the office of the sole member of staff. That member of staff had the rank and pay of a Junior Porter. This was a cost saving measure on the part of the LVR. All staff at the intermediate stations had a similar rank, but at Great Shefford the man had the duty and responsibility of opening and closing the heavy gates at the level crossing.

As if that were not enough for the overworked Junior Porter, Great Shefford soon proved to be one of the busier stations along the line. Local dairy farmers deposited surprisingly large numbers of milk churns on the platform to be collected by the morning and evening trains. One farm alone shipped out 200 gallons a day. Another bulky freight export, though one that was only seasonal, was straw. Large numbers of straw bales were taken out in the spring to go to the strawberry fields of Hampshire. There the straw was put down to keep the

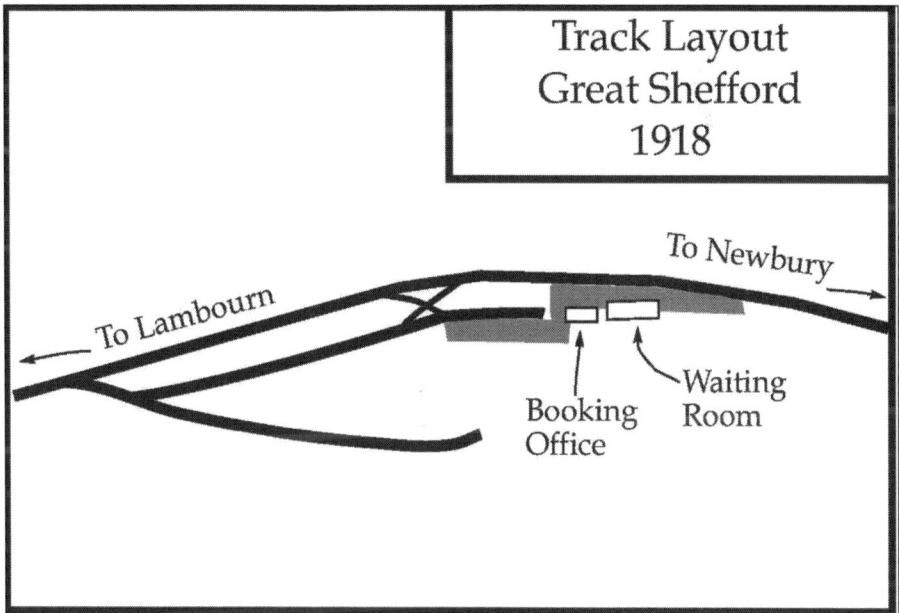

Track Layout
Great Shefford
1918

To Newbury

To Lambourn

Booking Office

Waiting Room

41

strawberries off the wet earth and to trap the warmth of the sun, and so ripen the strawberries better.

There were also the usual passengers, light freight and coal using the station. Finally the platform was used by timber cutters to move out their products.

When the GWR took over the line in 1905, a coal siding was installed for the use of coal merchants serving the surrounding villages. The platform was rebuilt so that it was more suitable for all weather use, and was considerably enlarged. There was a special bay platform put in for the loading of freight, particularly the timber. By 1914 the station was so busy that the GWR hired a second porter to aid what until then had been a sole member of staff. The two men worked separate shifts that ran from 7am to 9pm and overlapped in the middle of the day.

In 1923 a new crane was installed at the not inconsiderable cost of £179 specifically for the use of the timber trade. It had a lifting capacity of 64 tons, which was more than enough. Despite such improvements the amount of passengers and freight using Great Shefford and other stations on the line decreased after World War 2. The station closed in 1960.

There is almost nothing to see at Great Shefford Railway Station today. The demolition crews were very thorough. The site of the station is accessible. It lies at the end of the aptly named Station Road, which turns north off the A338 immediately south of the bridge over the Lambourn. Walk up Station Road for fifty yards. Then turn right to cross the river. At this point Station Road narrows dramatically to run up the side of Mill House. Continue up the narrow road to its end. In front of you and to your left you will find a playing field complete with children's playground. This is the site of the station. The main platform stood underneath and ran west from the playground while the coalyard was to the southwest where bushes and scrub now grow.

East Garston Station
The name of East Garston is something of a misnomer for there is no West Garston anywhere to be found in Berkshire. In fact the name derives from Asgarston, or Asgar's Tun. In 1066 the mill, farms and land (tun) here belonged to a man named Asgar, so the area was dubbed "Asgar's Tun".

This Asgar did not own only this patch of land, but extensive acres around Berkshire and Wiltshire. He was the chief horse buyer for King Edward the Confessor and when that king died transferred his loyalty to the new King Harold Godwinson. Asgar was with Harold at the Battle of Hastings and although he escaped the massacre that followed Harold's death he was badly wounded protecting the royal banner of England. Such a military role suited Asgar's name which means "Spear of God". Over time Asgar's Tun became East Garston, but there never was a West Garston.

The line from Newbury entered the Lambourn Valley at Speen, then headed northwest keeping close to the river to achieve the shallowest slope possible and to avoid the need for expensive cuttings and embankments. Between Great Shefford and East Garston the line rose at an average gradient of 1:82 as it passed Maidencourt Farm, but then levelled out flat for the final few hundred yards to East Garston. At the village, the line swung north of the village and the station was built beside the lane that led from the village to the church, manor house and some outlying farms.

The original station was rudimentary. The platform was only 9 inches tall and served more to keep passengers' feet dry in bad weather than anything else. A wooden shed, grandly dubbed an "office" stood at the western end of the platform beside the access from Church Road, soon to be renamed Station Road. A level crossing operated over the road, and the operation of this was the responsibility of the sole member of staff.

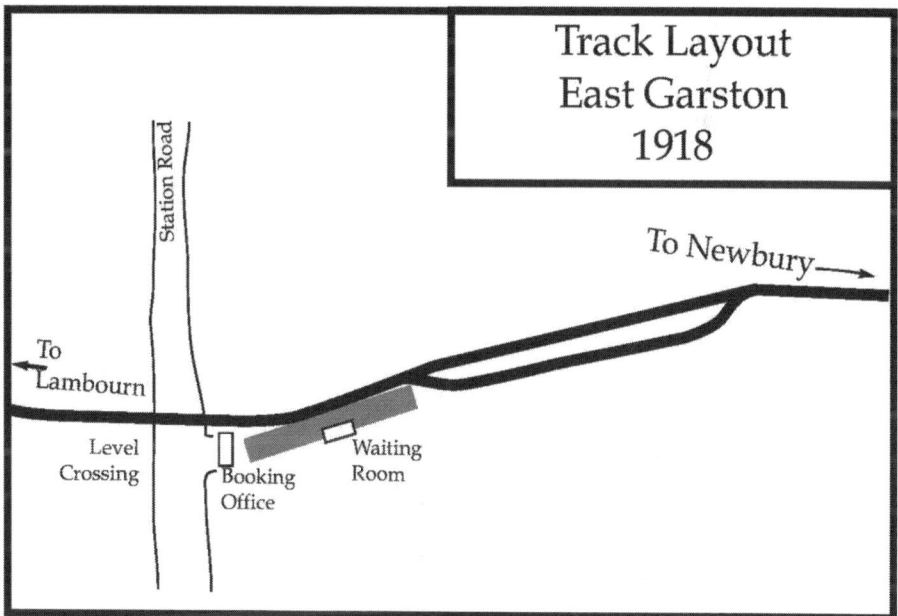

Track Layout
East Garston
1918

To Newbury

To Lambourn

Station Road

Level Crossing

Booking Office

Waiting Room

As at other LVR stations, this man had the rank and pay of Junior Porter. As well as working the level crossing he had to assist passengers, manhandle freight and light the two oil lamps that illuminated the platform after dark. The junior porter was given a smart uniform which consisted of a three piece suit with a long, cutaway jacket, a peaked cap and stout boots.

After the takeover by the GWR, the station was gradually rebuilt. The platform was raised to a more usual height and given a proper passenger shelter for bad weather. The old "office" remained, though it was improved and enlarged. The main freight business from East Garston had become milk, with churns being left on the platform by farmers to be collected by the morning and evening trains. The GWR felt its passengers deserved better than to negotiate milk churns on the platform, so a special milk loading dock was installed on the opposite side of the line. Other goods were to be stored at the far end of the platform from the road in a small yard. Finally a loop was installed at the eastern end of the station.

This newly improved East Garston station was, in 1913, taken over by Tom Liddiard who was given the newly enhanced position of Porter. Tom found that he had quite a bit of time on his hands between trains and, being a keen gardener, decided to do a bit of planting to brighten up his station. What began as a hobby developed into a passion. East Garston not only had neatly trimmed lawns and carefully tended flower beds, but climbing roses and other flowers were trained up and over the office, the waiting room and even the station sign board. The GWR ran a competition each year to find the best blooms at a station, and Tom Liddiard won it several times. He remained in his job at East Garston throughout his working life and retired, still as a Porter at East Garston in 1957. Just three years later the station closed.

The site of the East Garston Station can be found easily enough. From the village centre take Station Road heading toward the church. Just before you reach the church the road is crossed by a footpath signed left to Lambourn and right to Great Shefford. This path follows the route of the old railway. The station stood to the right or east side of the road. The site of the platform can be seen in the shape of an elongated mound with trees beyond. This footpath is part of the Lambourn Valley Way, a long distance path that runs from Uffington to Newbury.

Eastbury Station

The village of Eastbury has never been particularly large. Back in 1086 it did not even rate a separate entry in the Domesday Book but was simply grouped in with

Lambourn. Throughout its existence the village relied for its prosperity on the sheep that grazed the upland downs that spread out to both north and south. The small fields that were ploughed, and the gardens where fruit and vegetables were grown, relied for fertiliser on sheep dung brought down from the hills.

The line from Newbury entered the Lambourn Valley at Speen and then ran up the valley keeping as close to the river as possible and hugging the contours to avoid the need for expensive cuttings and embankments. Leaving East Garston, the line had barely a mile to go to reach Eastbury. The first few hundred yards were, for this line, a steepish climb at a gradient of 1:60, but then the line entered a longer shallow descent at 1:200.

The original station erected by the LBV was rudimentary even by the fairly basic standards of the line. The platform was the standard 9 inches tall but there was no fencing and no shelter for passengers. This latter ommission led to complaints from passengers, so the LVR hired a local carpenter to knock up a shelter. This took the form of a wooden shed with a simple sloping roof and an open doorway without a door, with a bench inside. At least it kept the rain off.

The reasons for the basic provision was that the population of the village was only 254, so little by way of passenger numbers were expected. Moreover the stations of East Garston and Lambourn were each less than two miles away. In fact the main reason that there was a station here at all was the Baylis Dairy Farm. This farm produced large quantities of milk, all of which was to be taken out by the LVR. There were usually more milk churns on the platform at Eastbury than there were passengers. When the GWR took over they raised the platform, but the wooden shed remained the only shelter however. Remarkably it remained in position until 1959 though it was by then much patched and repaired.

Eastbury was never a busy station, even by branch line standards. The timetable reflected this for several trains did not stop here. On Mondays, Tuesdays, Wednesdays and Fridays only three trains stopped at Eastbury. On Thursdays, market day in Newbury, an extra train stopped here and on Saturdays no less than five trains called. Sunday services were erratic with drivers stopping if they saw milk churns for collection or if flagged down by a passenger. The station closed entirely in 1960, along with all other stations north of Welford Park.

There is not much to see at Eastbury to remind the visitor that a station once stood here, though the site is easy enough to find. From the Plough Inn in Eastbury walk southeast to a crossroads, turn left up the lane that leads past a large thatched barn to Eastbury Grange up on the hills. After a hundred yards or

Lambourn Station in the 1930s photographed from the northwest. The main passenger platform is the roofed structure and platform to the centre left of the photo. The white building to the right is the goods shed. The siding that had run to the now demolished engine shed is between the two.

so the lane is flanked by the large brick abutments of what was once the bridge that carried the railway over the road. immediately before the abutments, take the path left, up a flight of concrete steps to climb up on to the old railway embankment. Once up on the embankment follow the path past the backs of domestic gardens and farm buildings to where an open field lies off to the left. The station used to stand here, but other than a rise in the ground indicating where the platform used to be there is nothing to see.

Lambourn Station
The name of the village derives from the Saxon for "Lamb Wash" and probably indicates that lambs were washed here and inspected for parasites or health problems before being turned out to graze on the downs. The name indicates just how important sheep were to the village at this time, and they have remained a major resource ever since.

The Lambourn Valley Railway opened for business on Monday 4 April 1898, with all the working buildings and facilities at Lambourn. The space chosen was located 200 yards from the village centre where there was a fairly broad flat area of ground close to the Bockhampton Road. Workmen began hacking away at the slope of Coppington Hill to dig down to the level of the station. The excavated chalk was then used to build up the lower slopes, being retained in position by a wall of solid granite blocks some six feet tall. The extensive flat area thus created was accessed off the Bockhampton Road by a steeply sloping road, named Station Road, that led up to a gateway almost 16 feet wide. This was blocked by a gate when the station was not open.

The main line from Newbury came in and formed the northern edge of the terminus. It ran along the southside of the platform, which was equipped with a proper station building in the form of a wooden house with offices and ticket office - the only such building on the entire line. This line had a loop on its south side to allow the locomotive that had hauled the train into Lambourn to decouple,

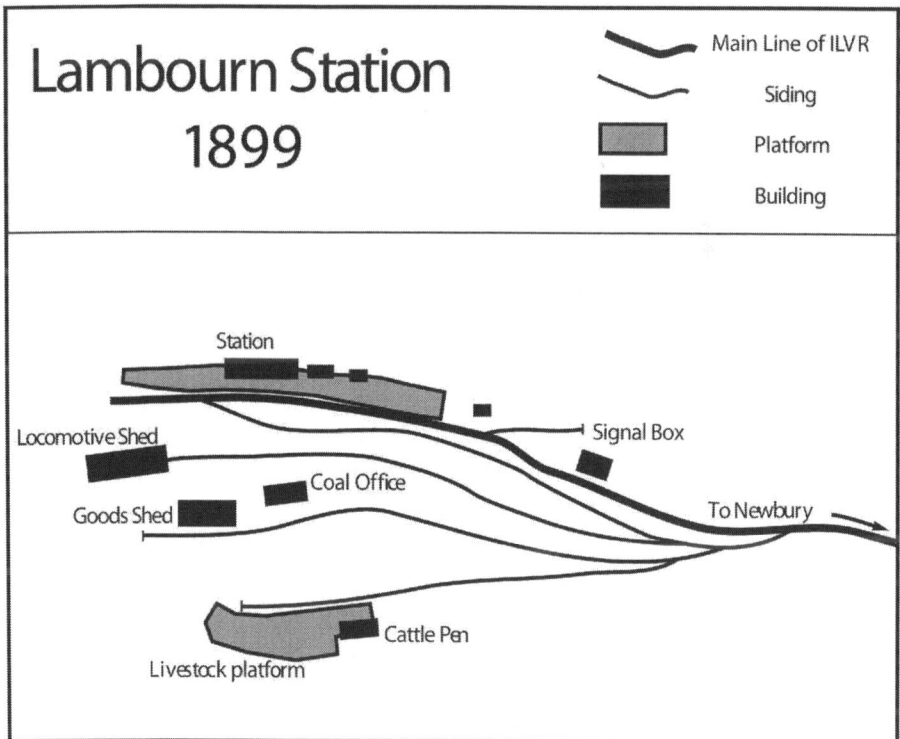

Lambourn Station 1899

Main Line of ILVR
Siding
Platform
Building

Station
Locomotive Shed
Signal Box
Coal Office
Goods Shed
To Newbury
Cattle Pen
Livestock platform

the GWR erected a proper platform of bricks and topped by cinders that stood to a more normal height, allowing passengers to simply step straight on to a carriage. There was also an imposing brick-built station building with overhanging canopy that sheltered almost half the platform. There was even a fireplace in the waiting room to keep passengers warm in chilly weather. Further along the new platform were a pair of wooden sheds for storage of equipment.

The goods sidings also came in for improvement. The tracks were relaid as standard GWR rails. The old wooden water tank was replaced with one of metal. The coal loading dock was provided with a canopy and a dedicated coal office was built, albeit in the form of a wooden shed. The livestock loading dock was enlarged and raised to wagon height so that the racehorses could step straight in to their horseboxes instead of having to climb a ramp.

The only building that the GWR found redundant was the engine shed. While the LVR had operated out of Lambourn, the GWR ran the line with engines and rolling stock from Newbury. The stoutly built shed was too good to be demolished, however, so it was retained until it became run down when it was taken away. The engine shed siding was then used to store surplus rolling stock until it was needed. The GWR retained this layout throughout its ownership of the station.

Lambourn Station was stripped of rails, points and anything else that British Railways thought it could use elsewhere. The site was then turned over to use as a storage yard and for light industrial uses. In the 1990s it was redeveloped for housing and the site is now occupied by a cul-de-sac of houses named "The Old Station Yard." Apart from the name there is no sign at all that a railway terminus ever stood here.